Why Christmas?

THE CHRISTMAS EDITION OF WHY JESUS?

NICKY GUMBEL

Illustrated by Charlie Mackesy

ALPHA PUBLICATIONS

First edition of Why Jesus? published by Kingsway Publications Ltd
in 1991. The Christmas edition first published 1995.

This edition published by Alpha International.
Reprinted 1998 (twice), 2000 (twice), 2001, 2002 (twice), 2003.

ISBN 1 898838 46 1

Biblical quotations are from the New International Version,
© 1973, 1978, 1984 by the International Bible Society.
Inclusive language version.

Published by Alpha International
Holy Trinity Brompton, Brompton Road, London, SW7 1JA

Illustrations by Charlie Mackesy

WHY CELEBRATE CHRISTMAS?

There is something almost magical about Christmas: children dream of Father Christmas and his fantasy sleigh, we picture Christmas trees, snowy scenes, filled-up stockings, piles of presents and smiling families around the fire.

The reality is often not as perfect as we imagine. Some people go over the top at Christmas. The overcrowding on the streets and in the shops can lead to so-called 'Santa-Claustrophobia'.

Over-indulging takes its toll on family life. One nine year-old boy wrote, 'I know Christmas should be a religious time, but to me Christmas is a time for the necessities of life such as food, presents and booze.' Another boy wrote, 'After breakfast we go into the sitting-room. Dad comes in drunk with Mum's tights and an Indian hat on!'
His teacher wrote in the margin, 'Good old Dad!'

For some, there is a danger of over-spending - buying presents that others do not need with money they have not got.

One little girl wrote to her granny, 'Thank you very much for the nice gloves you sent me for Christmas. They were something I wanted - but not very much!'

Others can become over-demanding. One doting father asked his small daughter well in advance what she would like for Christmas. Shyly she announced she would like a baby brother. To everyone's surprise and delight her mother returned from hospital on Christmas Eve with a baby boy in her arms. When the father repeated the question next year, there was less hesitation. 'If it wouldn't be too uncomfortable for Mummy, I would like a pony!'

But while some go over the top, others go under. For many, Christmas is one of the worst times of the year. Suicide rates go up, more people die from 'natural causes', marriages fall apart, psychiatrists' patients suffer regressions and family feuds begin.

One Mori poll suggested that there are three million family rows each Christmas. A newspaper article, headed, 'Enough to drive you crackers', spoke of people cracking up at Christmas as a result of the pressure to be perfect. It reported that two psychologists, a psychotherapist and a counsellor were running a workshop entitled 'Stress in the family: coping with Christmas'. They said that part of its success seemed to be the chance it

offered to get away from it all. The psychiatrist, Anthony Storr, in an article on depression at Christmas entitled, 'Cheer up, it's soon over' had this final piece of advice: 'Remember that Christmas, although recurrent, doesn't last for ever.'

With all the magic, the stress and the hype of Christmas, are we missing the point? What is at the heart of Christmas? In the words of C.S.Lewis, at Christmas we remember the 'central event in the history of the earth - the very thing the whole story has been about'.

WHY BOTHER WITH JESUS?

When Jesus was born a group of highly intelligent philosophers thought he was worth bothering with. They stopped everything to take him three symbolic presents. The first was gold - a present fit for a king. The child in the manger was the King of kings and

Lord of lords. God himself had come to live as part of our world.

Too often Jesus has been obscured by Christmas. One man wrote to *The Times*: 'Sir: Failing to find any religious books in the bookshop, I asked an assistant for help. She showed me an inconspicuous handful of Bibles and prayer books, saying: "We have had to move them down to the bottom shelf because of Christmas"'.

But the point of Christmas is Jesus Christ. At Christmas we celebrate the birthday of the most important person who has ever lived. He is the centrepiece of our civilisation. After all, we call what happened before his birth 'BC' and what happened after 'AD'.

But how do we know it is true?

We can test the claims of Christianity because it is an historical faith. It is based on the life, death and resurrection of Jesus Christ. Our faith is based on firm historical evidence.

Who is Jesus?

Jesus was and is the Son of God. Some people think

he was just a 'good religious teacher'. However, that suggestion does not fit with the facts.

a) *His claims*

Jesus claimed to be the unique Son of God - on an equal footing with God. He assumed the authority to forgive sins. He said that one day he would judge the world and that what would matter then would be how we had responded to him in this life.

C.S. Lewis pointed out that:
'A man who was merely a man and said the sort of things Jesus said would not be a great moral teacher.' He would either be insane or else he would be 'the Devil of Hell'. 'You must make your choice,' he writes. Either Jesus was, and is, the Son of God or else he was insane or evil but, C.S. Lewis goes on, 'let us not come up with any patronising nonsense about his being a great human teacher. He has not left that open to us. He did not intend to.'

b) *His character*

Many people who do not profess to be Christians regard Jesus as the supreme example of a selfless life. Dostoevsky, himself a Christian, said, 'I believe there is no one lovelier, deeper, more sympathetic and more perfect than Jesus. I say to myself, with jealous love, that not only is there no one else like him but there could never be anyone like him.'

As far as his teaching is concerned, there seems to be general agreement that it is the purest and best ever to have fallen from human lips.

As C.S. Lewis put it, 'It seems obvious that he was neither a lunatic nor a fiend; and consequently, however strange or terrifying or unlikely it may seem, I have to accept the view that he was and is God. God has landed on this enemy occupied world in human form.'

c) *His conquest of death*

The evidence for the physical resurrection is very strong indeed. When the disciples went to the tomb they found that the grave clothes had collapsed and that Jesus' body was absent.

In the next six weeks he was seen by over 500 people. The disciples' lives were transformed and the Christian Church was born, and then grew at a dynamic rate.

A former Lord Chief Justice of England, Lord Darling, said of the resurrection: 'In its favour as living truth there exists such overwhelming evidence, positive and negative, factual and circumstantial, that no intelligent jury in the world could fail to bring in a verdict that the resurrection story is true.' The only satisfactory explanation for these facts is that Jesus did indeed rise from the dead and thus confirms that he was, and is, the Son of God.

The wise men were right. Nothing less than gold would be suitable for such a child.

WHY DO WE NEED HIM?

Even if Jesus was who he said he was, why do we need him 2,000 years later? The second gift the wise men brought was frankincense, which was used in the temple as the symbol of prayer, and pointed to a relationship with God.

Relationships are exciting. They are the most important aspect of our lives - our relationships with our parents, boyfriend or girlfriend, husband or wife, children, grandchildren, friends, and so on.

Christianity is first and foremost about relationships rather than rules. It is about a Person more than a philosophy. It is about the most important relationship of all: our relationship with the God who made us. Jesus said that the first and greatest commandment is to love God. The second is to love

our neighbour. So, it is also about our relationships with other people.

You and I were created to live in a relationship with God. Until we find that relationship there will always be something missing in our lives. As a result, we are often aware of a gap. One rock singer described it by saying: 'I've got an emptiness deep inside.' One woman, in a letter to me, wrote of 'a deep deep void'. Another young girl spoke of 'a chunk missing in her soul'.

People try to fill this emptiness in various ways. Some try to close the gap with money, but that does not satisfy. Aristotle Onassis, who was one of the richest men in the world, said at the end of his life: 'Millions do not always add up to what a man needs out of life'.

Others try drugs or excess alcohol or sexual promiscuity. One girl said to me, 'These things provide instant gratification but they leave you feeling hollow afterwards.' Still others try hard work, music, sport or seek success. There may not be anything wrong with these in themselves but they do not satisfy that hunger deep inside every human being.

Even the closest human relationships, wonderful though they are, do not in themselves satisfy this 'emptiness deep inside'. Nothing will fill this gap except the relationship with God for which we were made.

According to the New Testament, the reason for this emptiness is that men and women have turned their backs on God.

Jesus said, 'I am the bread of life' (John 6:35). He is the only one who can satisfy our deepest hunger because he is the one who makes it possible for our relationship with God to be restored.

a) *He satisfies our hunger for meaning and purpose in life*

At some point everyone asks the question, 'What am I doing on earth?' or, 'What is the point of life?' or, 'Is there any purpose to life?' As Albert Camus once said, 'Man cannot live without meaning.'

Until we are living in a relationship with God we will never find the true meaning and purpose of life. Other things may provide passing satisfaction but it does not last. Only in a relationship with our Creator do we find the true meaning and purpose of our lives.

b) *He satisfies our hunger for life beyond death*

Before I was a Christian I did not like to think about the subject of death. My own death seemed a long way in the future. I did not know what would happen and I did not want to think about it. I was failing to face up to reality. The fact is that we will all die. Yet God has 'set eternity in the human heart' (Ecclesiastes 3:11). Most people do not want to die. We long to survive beyond death. Only in Jesus Christ do we find eternal life. For our relationship with God, which starts now, survives death and goes on into eternity.

c) *He satisfies our hunger for forgiveness*

If we are honest, we would have to admit that we all do things that we know are wrong. Sometimes we do things of which we are deeply ashamed. More than that, there is a self-centredness about our lives which spoils them. Jesus said, 'What comes out of you is what makes you "unclean". For from within, out of your hearts, come evil thoughts, sexual immorality, theft, murder, adultery, greed, malice, deceit, lewdness, envy, slander, arrogance and folly. All these evils come from inside and make you "unclean"' (Mark 7:20-23).

Our greatest need, in fact, is for forgiveness. Just as someone who has cancer needs a doctor whether they realise it or not, so we need forgiveness whether we realise it or not. Just as with cancer, those who recognise their need are far better off than those who are lulled into a false sense of security.

By his death on the cross Jesus made it possible for us to be forgiven and brought back into a relationship with God.

At Christmas we remember the fact that Jesus entered our world in order to restore relationships - first our relationship with God and then our relationships with others. In this way he supplied the answer to our deepest need.

WHY DID HE COME?

Why did Jesus come? How could he achieve this restoration of our relationship with God? The third present the wise men brought gives us the answer. Myrrh was used to embalm the bodies of the dead. Jesus is the only man who has ever chosen to be born and he is one of the few who has chosen to die. He said that the entire reason for his coming was to die for us. He came 'to give his life as a ransom for many' (Mark 10:45). The supreme reason for giving Christmas presents is to remind us of his gift to us - the most valuable and expensive gift ever given.

From what we know of crucifixion it was one of the cruellest forms of execution. Cicero described it as 'the most cruel and hideous of tortures'. Jesus would have been flogged with a whip of several strands of leather weighted with pieces of metal and bones. According to Eusebius, a third-century historian, 'The sufferer's veins were laid bare, and the very muscles, sinews and bowels of the victim were opened to exposure.' Jesus was then forced to carry a six-foot cross beam until he collapsed. When he reached the site of execution, six-inch nails were hammered through his wrists and feet as he was nailed to the cross. He was left to hang for hours in excruciating pain.

Yet, the New Testament makes it clear that there was something worse for Jesus than the physical and emotional pain; this was the spiritual anguish of being separated from God as he carried all our sins.

Why did he die?

Jesus said he died 'for' us. The word 'for' means 'instead of'. He did it because he loved us and did not want us to have to pay the penalty for all the things that we had done wrong. On the cross he was effectively saying, 'I will take all those things on myself.'

He did it for you and he did it for me. If you or I had been the only person in the world he would have done it for us. St. Paul wrote of 'the Son of God, who loved me and gave himself for me' (Galatians 2:20). It was out of love for us that he gave his life as a ransom.

The word 'ransom' comes from the slave market. A kind person might buy a slave and set him free - but first the ransom price had to be paid. Jesus paid, by his blood on the cross, the ransom price to set us free.

Freedom from what?

a) *Freedom from guilt*

Whether we feel guilty or not, we are all guilty before God because of the many times we have broken his laws in thought, word and deed. Just as when someone commits a crime there is a penalty to be paid, so there is a penalty for breaking God's law. 'The wages of sin is death' (Romans 6:23). The result of the things we do wrong is spiritual death - being cut off from God eternally. We all deserve to suffer that penalty. On the cross Jesus took the penalty in our place so that we could be totally forgiven and our guilt could be taken away.

b) *Freedom from addiction*

Jesus said that 'everyone who sins is a slave to sin' (John 8:34). Jesus died to set us free from that slavery. On the cross, the power of this addiction was broken. Although we may still fall from time to time, the power of this addiction is broken when Jesus sets us free. That is why Jesus went on to say that 'if the Son sets you free you will be free indeed' (John 8:36).

c) *Freedom from fear*

Jesus came so that 'by his death he might destroy him who holds the power of death - that is, the devil - and free those who all their lives were held in slavery by their fear of death' (Hebrews 2:14-15).

13

We need no longer fear death. Death is not the end for those whom Jesus has set free. Rather it is the gateway to heaven, where we will be free from even the presence of sin. When Jesus set us free from the fear of death, he also set us free from all other fears.

Freedom for what?

Jesus is no longer physically on earth but he has not left us alone. He has sent his Holy Spirit to be with us. When his Spirit comes to live within us, he gives us a new freedom.

a) *Freedom to know God*

The things which we do wrong cause a barrier between us and God: 'Your iniquities have separated you from your God' (Isaiah 59:2). When Jesus died on the cross he removed the barrier that existed between us and God. As a result he has made it possible for us to have a relationship with our Creator. We become his sons and daughters. The Spirit assures us of this relationship and he helps us to get to know God better. He helps us to pray and to understand God's word (the Bible).

b) *Freedom to love*

'We love because he first loved us' (1 John 4:19). As we look at the cross we understand God's love for us. When the Spirit of God comes to live within us we experience that love. As we do so we receive a new love for God and for other people. We are set free to live a life of love - a life centred around loving and serving Jesus and loving and serving other people rather than a life centred around ourselves.

c) Freedom to change

People sometimes say, 'You are what you are. You can't change.' The good news is that with the help of the Spirit we can change. The Holy Spirit gives us the freedom to live the sort of lives that deep down we have always wanted to live. St. Paul tells us that the fruit of the Spirit is 'love, joy, peace, patience, kindness, goodness, faithfulness, gentleness and self-control' (Galatians 5:22). When we ask the Spirit of God to come and live within us, these wonderful characteristics begin to grow in our lives.

WHY NOT?

So God offers us in Christ Jesus forgiveness, freedom and his Spirit to live within us. All this is a gift from God. When someone offers us a present we have a choice. We can either accept it, open it and enjoy it. Or else we can say, 'No thank you.' Sadly, many people make excuses for not accepting the gift which God offers.

Here are some of the excuses:

a) *'I have no need of God'*

When people say this they usually mean that they are quite happy without God. What they fail to realise is that our greatest need is not 'happiness' but 'forgiveness'. It takes a very proud person to say that they have no need of forgiveness.

We all need forgiveness. Without it we are in serious trouble. For God is not only our loving Father; he is also a righteous judge.

Either we accept what Jesus has done for us on the cross, or else one day we will pay the just penalty ourselves for the things we have done wrong.

b) *'There is too much to give up'*

Sometimes, God puts his finger
on something in our lives
which we know is wrong
and which we would have
to give up if we want
to enjoy this
relationship
with God
through Jesus.

But we need to remember:-

❏ God loves us. He asks us only to
give up things which do us harm.
If I saw some small children playing
with a carving knife I would tell
them to stop, not because I want to
ruin their fun but because I do
not want them to get hurt.

❏ What we give up is nothing
compared to what we receive.
The cost of not becoming a
Christian is far greater than the
cost of becoming a Christian.

❏ What we give up is nothing
compared to what Jesus gave
up when he died on the cross for us.

c) *'There must be a trap'*

Understandably, people often find it hard to accept that there is anything free in this life. They think it all sounds too easy and that there must be some hidden trap. However, what they fail to realise is that although it is free for us, it was not free for Jesus. He paid for it with his own blood. It is easy for us, but it was not easy for him.

d) *'I'm not good enough'*

None of us is good enough. Nor can we ever make ourselves good enough for God. But that is why Jesus came. He made it possible for God to accept us just as we are, whatever we have done and however much of a mess we have made of our lives.

e) *'I could never keep it up'*

We are right to think that we could never keep it up. We cannot by ourselves, but the Spirit of God, who comes to live within us, gives us the power and the strength to keep going as Christians.

f) *'I'll do it later'*

This is perhaps the most common excuse. Sometimes people say, 'I know it's true but I'm not ready.' They put it off. The longer we put it off the harder it becomes and the more we miss out. We never know whether we will get another opportunity. Speaking for myself, my only regret is that I did not accept the gift earlier.

WHAT DO WE HAVE TO DO?

The New Testament makes it clear that we have to do something to accept the gift that God offers. This is an act of faith. John writes that 'God so loved the world that he gave his one and only Son that whoever believes in him shall not perish but have eternal life' (John 3:16). Believing involves an act of faith, based on all that we know about Jesus. It is not blind faith. It is putting our trust in a Person. In some ways it is like the step of faith taken by a bride or a bridegroom when they say, 'I will' on their wedding day.

The way people take this step of faith varies enormously but I want to describe one way in which you can take this step of faith right now. It can be summarised by three very simple words:

a) *'Sorry'*

You have to ask God to forgive you for all the things you have done wrong and turn from everything which you know is wrong in your life. This is what the Bible means by 'repentance'.

b) *'Thank you'*

We believe that Jesus died for us on the cross. You need to thank him for dying for you and for the offer of his free gift of forgiveness, freedom and his Spirit.

c) *'Please'*

God never forces his way into our lives. You need to accept his gift and invite him to come and live within you by his Spirit.

If you would like to have a relationship with God and you are ready to say these three things, then here is a very simple prayer which you can pray and which will be the start of that relationship:

> Lord Jesus Christ,
>
> I am sorry for the things I have done wrong in my life (take a few moments to ask his forgiveness for anything particular that is on your conscience). Please forgive me. I now turn from everything which I know is wrong.
>
> Thank you that you died on the cross for me so that I could be forgiven and set free.
>
> Thank you that you offer me forgiveness and the gift of your Spirit. I now receive that gift.
>
> Please come into my life by your Holy Spirit to be with me forever.
>
> Thank you, Lord Jesus. Amen.

WHAT NOW?

1. *Tell someone*

   It is important to tell someone in order to underline the decision you have made. Often it is only when you tell someone else that it becomes a reality to you. It is probably best to start by telling someone who you think will be pleased to hear the news.

2. *Read the Bible*

Once we have received Jesus and put our trust in him we become children of God. He is our heavenly Father. Like any father he wants us to have a close relationship with him. We develop this relationship as we listen to him (primarily through the Bible) and as we speak to him in prayer. The Bible is the word of God and you might find it helpful to begin by reading a few verses of John's gospel every day. Ask God to speak to you as you read.

3. *Start to speak to God each day (ie. pray)*

I find the following a great help:

       A -   Adoration
              Praising God for who he is and what he has done.

       C -   Confession
              Asking God's forgiveness for anything that we have done wrong.

       T -   Thanksgiving
              Thanking God for health, family, friends and so on.

       S -   Supplication
              Praying for ourselves, for our friends and for others.

4. *Join a lively church*

It is important to be part of a group of Christians who get together to worship God, to hear what God is saying to them, to encourage one another and to make friends. Church should be an exciting place!

I first prayed a prayer like the one on page 20 on 16 February, 1974. It changed my life. It is the best and most important thing I have ever done. I trust it will be the same for you.

Further reading: *Questions of Life* by Nicky Gumbel, which looks in greater detail at the relevance of Jesus to our lives today.